fic
phone

Word

37906

Word Bird  Bird™

Makes Words With Duck

The Child's World

Published in the United States of America by The Child's World®, Inc.
PO Box 326
Chanhassen, MN 55317-0326
800-599-READ
www.childsworld.com

Project Manager Mary Berendes
Editor Katherine Stevenson, Ph.D.
Designer Ian Butterworth

Library of Congress Cataloging-in-Publication Data
Moncure, Jane Belk.
Word Bird makes words with Duck : a short "u" adventure / by Jane Belk Moncure.
p. cm.
Summary: On a rainy day Word Bird makes up words with his friend
Duck, and each word that they make up leads them into a new activity.
ISBN 1-56766-901-8 (lib. bdg.)
[1. Vocabulary. 2. Birds—Fiction. 3. Ducks—Fiction.] I. Title.
PZ7.M739 Wne 2001
[E]—dc21
00-010896

Word Bird™

Makes Words
With Duck

by Jane Belk Moncure

illustrated by Chris McEwan

One rainy day, Word Bird made word puzzles…

under an umbrella.

Word Bird put

d with uck.

What did Word Bird make?

duck

Just then, Duck came over to play.

"I can make word puzzles, too," said Duck.

Duck put

s   with   un.

What word did Duck make?

s un

Just then, the sun
came out.

Word Bird put down
the umbrella.

But then the thunder
rumbled!

Word Bird put the
umbrella up again.

"What can we do?" asked
Duck. Word Bird put

dr with um.

What did Word Bird make?

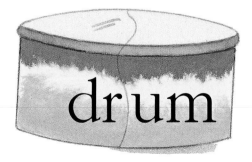

drum

"I have a drum," said
Word Bird.

"Let's play your drum," said
Duck. They played.

Tum-tum-tum!
Tum-tum-tum!

The thunder rumbled.
Bum-bum!

And tum-tum
went the drum.

Then the sun came out.

Word Bird put the umbrella down again.

"What can we do now?"
asked Duck. Word Bird put

tr with uck.

What did Word Bird make?

tr uck

"Let's play with my truck," said Word Bird. "I have a dump truck."

Duck found a mud puddle.

"Let's put mud in the dump truck," Duck said.

They filled the dump truck with mud. Then they dumped the mud.

"Let's make mud pies,"
said Duck.

They made lots of mud
pies. "The sun will dry the
mud pies," said Duck.

"Let's jump over the mud
puddle," said Word Bird.
But…

Word Bird jumped into
the mud!

Word Bird was stuck
in the mud.

Duck pulled Word Bird out.

"You must jump very high so you will not get stuck in the mud," said Duck.

Suddenly, it began to thunder again. Word Bird put up the umbrella.

"What can we do now?" asked Duck.

Word Bird put

b with us.

What did Word Bird make?

b us

"I have a little bus," said
  Word Bird.

"I will be the bus driver,"
  Word Bird said.

"No, no!" said Duck.
"I will be the bus driver."

Then they had a fuss.

"Let's take turns,"
said Word Bird.

"You drive the bus.
Then I will drive the bus."

The bus went bump-bump!

Duck stopped the bus.
Word Bird jumped out.
Word Bird picked a bunch
of buttercups for Duck.

Duck gave Word Bird
a hug.

You can read more word puzzles with Word Bird.

b ug

l umpy

c up

r ug

gr umpy

t ug

f un

g un

t ub

d umpy

bumpy

j umpy

Now you can make some word puzzles.